THE LITTLE BOOK OF
Biblical Justice

THE LITTLE BOOKS OF JUSTICE & PEACEBUILDING

Published titles include:

The Little Book of Restorative Justice, by Howard Zehr

El Pequeño Libro De Justicia Restaurativa, by Howard Zehr

The Little Book of Conflict Transformation, by John Paul Lederach

The Little Book of Family Group Conferences, New-Zealand Style, by Allan MacRae and Howard Zehr

The Little Book of Strategic Peacebuilding, by Lisa Schirch

The Little Book of Strategic Negotiation, by Jayne Seminare Docherty

The Little Book of Circle Processes, by Kay Pranis

The Little Book of Contemplative Photography, by Howard Zehr

The Little Book of Restorative Discipline for Schools, by Lorraine Stutzman Amstutz and Judy H. Mullet

The Little Book of Trauma Healing, by Carolyn Yoder

The Little Book of Biblical Justice, by Chris Marshall

The Little Book of Restorative Justice for People in Prison, by Barb Toews

The Little Book of Cool Tools for Hot Topics, by Ron Kraybill and Evelyn Wright

The Little Book of Dialogue for Difficult Subjects, by Lisa Schirch and David Campt

The Little Book of Victim Offender Conferencing, by Lorraine Stutzman Amstutz

The Little Book of Healthy Organizations, by David R. Brubaker and Ruth Hoover Zimmerman

---

The Little Books of Justice & Peacebuilding present, in highly accessible form, key concepts and practices from the fields of restorative justice, conflict transformation, and peacebuilding. Written by leaders in these fields, they are designed for practitioners, students, and anyone interested in justice, peace, and conflict resolution.

The Little Books of Justice & Peacebuilding series is a cooperative effort between the Center for Justice and Peacebuilding of Eastern Mennonite University (Howard Zehr, Series General Editor) and publisher Good Books (Phyllis Pellman Good, Senior Editor).

THE LITTLE BOOK OF

Biblical Justice

A fresh approach to the
Bible's teachings on justice

CHRIS MARSHALL

Intercourse, PA 17534
800/762-7171
www.GoodBooks.com

For
Alan and Eleanor Kreider,
who continue to inspire.

ὁ γὰρ ἐν τούτῳ δουλεύων τῷ Χριστῷ εὐάρεστος τῷ θεῷ
(Romans 14:18)

Cover photograph by Howard Zehr.

Design by Dawn J. Ranck
THE LITTLE BOOK OF BIBLICAL JUSTICE
Copyright © 2005 by Good Books, Intercourse, PA 17534
International Standard Book Number: 978-1-56148-505-5
Library of Congress Catalog Card Number: 2005029815

Library of Congress Cataloging-in-Publication Data
Marshall, Christopher D.
   The little book of biblical justice : a fresh approach to the Bible's teachings on
justice / Chris Marshall.
      p. cm.
   ISBN 1-56148-505-5 (pbk.)
   1. Justice--Biblical teaching. I. Title.
   BS680.J8M37 2005
   241'.622--dc22   2005029815

Table of Contents

1.
What is Justice?

The purpose of this *Little Book* is to identify some characteristic features of the Bible's teaching on justice. Christians regard the Bible as a uniquely important source of guidance on matters of belief and practice. What the Bible has to say about justice therefore—both social justice and criminal justice—ought to be of great significance for Christian thought and action today.

The Bible also has had a profound impact on the development of Western culture in general. So exploring biblical perspectives on justice can help us appreciate some of the convictions and values that have helped shape Western political and judicial thought in general.

Yet coming to grips with biblical teaching on justice is by no means easy. There are many complexities to cope with.

- There is a *huge amount of data to deal with*. There are hundreds of texts in the Old and New Testaments which speak explicitly about justice, and hundreds more which refer to it implicitly. Justice is in fact one of the most frequently recurring topics in the Bible.

- The *data is also diverse*. Different biblical writers address different historical circumstances, and they sometimes take different positions on what justice entails (especially with respect to criminal justice). In this *Little Book* we will concentrate on broad areas of theological agreement among the writers. But we do well to remember that, especially on issues of justice, the difficulty is always in the detail.

- We also always need to remember that biblical reflection on justice takes place within a larger *cultural and religious worldview that is, in many respects, quite unlike that of contemporary secular society.* Understanding the justice dimension of biblical teaching requires us to cross over into a different world from our own, and this is never an easy thing to do.

Added to these factors are the complexities that surround the concept of justice itself. What actually *is* justice? Does justice have an objective existence, or is it simply the product of social agreement? Is there an unchanging essence to justice—such as fairness or equality or balance—or does it mean different things to different people in different settings? Where does justice come from? How is justice known? How should it be defined? What is the relationship between justice, love, and mercy?

These are all very difficult questions which we cannot explore in any detail here. But even without traversing the difficult terrain of moral and legal philosophy, it is evident from everyday discourse that justice is a paradoxical value.

The Justice Paradox

Justice is one of those ideas that combines tremendous emotional potency with a great deal of semantic ambiguity. It is both a self-evident reality and, at the same time, a highly disputed one. Let's consider each side of this paradox:

- On the one hand, we all have a strong intuitive sense of what justice is. We appeal to the criterion of justice all the time. We instinctively recognize when it has been violated. Even very young children have a powerful, innate sense of justice. Think of how often children complain that something is just so unfair! To declare some action or state of affairs to be unfair or unjust is to make one of the strongest moral condemnations available. And when individuals make this complaint, they usually assume that the injustice in question will be patently obvious to anyone who cares to look.

- But what appears obvious to one person is not always obvious to others. People may agree that justice is the fundamental principle to consider, but they frequently disagree on how the principle translates into practice. Some, for example, defend capital punishment as a matter of just deserts, a life for a life, the rebalancing of the scales of justice. Others decry it as an affront to human dignity, an awful imitation of the injustice it claims to denounce or correct.

  Or again, some consider it to be a matter of basic justice that women have the right to choose an abortion, since it is their bodies that are affected. For others, however, abortion is a deadly injustice to an unborn child, the unjustifiable taking of innocent human life.

  Similar disputes on justice litter human history, and there have been huge shifts in social consensus from age to age. Aristotle considered slavery to be compatible with, even essential to, a just society. For later British and American abolitionists, slavery was the very epitome of injustice.

So we have a paradoxical situation. We all know that justice is important, we all feel obligated towards the demands of justice, we all sense the primordial pull of justice.

But we cannot say exactly what justice is, or how best to define it, or why standards of justice vary so much through the centuries and across different cultures.

Key Conceptual Components

Obviously justice is not a straightforward or singular concept. Like love, justice is a generic or inclusive term embracing a variety of meanings and applications. This makes it very difficult to reduce justice to a simple, all-encompassing definition. Yet most expositions of justice seem to involve at least four key ingredients:

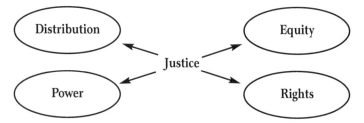

- *Distribution*: Justice entails the appropriate distribution of social benefits and penalties among contending parties. Justice dictates that people get their fair share in society's goods and rewards (social justice), and that they are not subjected to punishments or penalties unless they morally deserve them (criminal justice).

- *Power*: Justice involves the exercise of legitimate power—whether to arbitrate between conflicting claims, to implement social benefits, to enforce legal obligations, or to impose suitable sanctions. Injustice occurs when power is misused to deny or rob people of what they are rightfully due.

- *Equity:* Justice requires fairness and balance. Similars should be treated as similars, and dissimilars as dissimilars. Disputes should be adjudicated even-handedly, without regard to irrelevant, secondary considerations that would arbitrarily disadvantage one party.

- *Rights*: Justice has to do with honoring the rights or entitlements of people, especially in conflict situations. A right exists when someone has a legitimate moral or legal claim on some good, which others have a duty to respect or uphold. Justice gives moral legitimacy to such rights.

At the broadest level, then, justice entails the exercise of legitimate power to ensure that benefits and penalties are distributed fairly and equitably in society, thus meeting the rights and enforcing the obligations of all parties.

So far so good. Disputes arise when deciding questions like these: *Who* should exercise power? What *kind* of power is appropriate? *What* benefits or penalties do particular parties deserve? What constitutes a *fair* distribution of resources in view of the different characteristics and contributions of people? *Whose* rights take precedence when there is a clash between the legitimate rights or claims of various groups?

Making decisions in such disputes is never easy. It requires careful consideration of all the factors bearing on each situation. How these factors are distinguished and measured depends, in turn, on the larger worldview or belief system within which human communities operate. It is here that justice intersects with *religious* understandings and meanings. Those beliefs, values, stories, and symbols that make up a worldview are, by definition, religious in nature inasmuch as they presuppose or give answers to life's ultimate questions.

Most philosophers now agree that the content of justice cannot be determined simply through the exercise of objective, disembodied reason. No such faculty exists. Reason does not operate in splendid isolation from the rest of human experience. Human beings can only ever think about justice (or anything else for that matter) within the context of particular historical and cultural traditions. In other words, our reasoning, and thus our understanding of justice, is unavoidably contextual or historical in character. This need not mean that justice itself is merely the product of human reflection, that it has no objective, transcendent existence. It simply means that our knowledge of actual justice is always going to be limited and partial.

From a Christian perspective, justice *must* have a real objective existence, because justice derives from God, and God exists apart from human speculation. Justice is real because God is real. But our capacity to know God's universal justice is unavoidably conditioned by the ways of looking at life and the world which we receive from the particular historical and religious traditions to which we belong. This is where the Bible comes in.

The Bible's Contribution

Christians can be confident not only that justice exists because God exists, but that it is possible to know something substantial about the nature of justice, just as it is possible to know something substantial about the nature of God. And the place to learn about justice, first and foremost, is the biblical narrative of God's creative, sustaining, and redeeming activity in the world.

For the biblical writers, the meaning of justice is not discovered through abstract philosophical speculation. It is known primarily through God's revelation in history, and the biblical writings comprise the record of that revelation.

It is from the biblical story of God's self-disclosure, in both word and deed, that we can come to understand more of what justice entails.

We learn what justice is from the biblical story of God's self disclosure.

In the biblical narrative, two events stand out as uniquely important in understanding God's justice. The first is the *liberation* of the Hebrew slaves from Egypt and their formation into a covenant community living under God's law. Over and over again, the prophets and poets of Israel declare that God's justice has been made visible in this momentous intervention.

The second great event is the *coming of Jesus Christ,* who also brings deliverance from servitude and inaugurates a new covenant. For the New Testament writers, the Christ-event, even more than the exodus from Egypt, is the decisive "revelation of God's justice" (Romans 1:16-17; 3:21-26).

In between and around these two great events, the biblical writers speak eloquently and repeatedly of justice, both divine justice and human justice. Before trying to summarize what they say, a little more needs to be said about the theological worldview within which they talk of justice.

2.
Justice in the Biblical Worldview

This chapter sketches the understanding of justice that emerges from the wealth of biblical texts on the topic. This chapter also discusses some of the foundational convictions or core values of the biblical worldview that shapes its distinctive theology of justice. Many such beliefs or convictions could be mentioned, but five are notable for our purposes.

Foundations of biblical justice
   Shalom
   Covenant
   Torah
   Deed-Consequence
   Atonement-Forgiveness

However, before commenting on each of these ideas individually, it is important to reiterate just how central the theme of justice is in the Bible.

A Central Theme
Justice is one of the most frequently recurring topics in the Bible. For example, the main vocabulary items for sexual sin appear about 90 times in the Bible, while the major

Hebrew and Greek words for justice (*mishpat, sedeqah, diskaiosune, krisis*) occur over 1000 times.

Yet modern readers often fail to recognize how pervasive the notion of justice is in the Bible. This is partly because the key Hebrew and Greek terms are translated by a variety of English equivalents, some of which seem to us to lack any obvious connection with justice. This extensive English vocabulary is necessary because the biblical conception of justice is much bigger or more comprehensive than the current Western concept. Biblical justice touches on every aspect of life—the personal and the social, the public and the private, the political and the religious, the human and the nonhuman—and therefore requires a variety of translation terms to encompass its various applications. But the net effect of this is to obscure in the English text how widespread and interconnected the justice concept is in the original text.

The words for justice occur over 1000 times in the Bible.

Take the term "righteousness," for example, which occurs frequently in the Bible. The biblical language of righteousness refers broadly to "doing, being, declaring, or bringing about what is right." When it is used in contexts that deal with conflict, coercion, or social distribution, it often has the force of justice or justice-making. But in modern English usage, the terms "righteousness" and "justice" evoke very different connotations. Righteousness carries the sense of personal moral purity and religious piety, whereas justice relates to public judicial fairness and equality of rights. One belongs to the private, moral, religious realm, the other to the public, political, legal realm. But in biblical usage, righteousness includes what we mean by justice. Often in the Hebrew Bible, "righteousness" (*sedeqah*) and "justice" (*mishpat*) occur as a word-pair with virtually identical meanings:

> But let justice roll down like waters,
> and righteousness like an everflowing stream
> (Amos 5:24).

> See, a king will reign in righteousness,
> and princes will rule with justice (Isaiah 32:1).

> Give the king your justice, O God,
> and your righteousness to a king's son.
> May he judge your people with righteousness,
> and your poor with justice (Psalm 72:1-2).

So righteousness in the Bible incorporates the idea of doing justice, and doing justice in the Bible conveys the idea of righting what has gone wrong, of restoring things to a condition of "rightness" or righteousness.

It is sometimes said that the New Testament hardly ever speaks of justice. But that is simply wrong. Once we realize that the term righteousness belongs to the same field of meaning as justice, it becomes clear that the New Testament is no different from the Old Testament with respect to its focus on, and commitment to, the realization of justice.

A Complex of Related Ideas

- *Shalom*

    Shalom is the Hebrew word for "peace." But peace in the Bible is more than the negative absence of armed conflict or violence. Shalom denotes the positive presence of harmony and wholeness, of health and prosperity, of integration and balance. It is the state of soundness or flourishing in all dimensions of existence—in our relationship with God, our relationships with each another, our relationship with nature, and our relationship with ourselves.

In shalom, peace and justice go together. Shalom is when everything is as it ought to be. In this sense, shalom encapsulates God's basic intention for humanity—that people live in a condition of "all rightness" in every department of life.

Shalom thus combines in one concept the meaning of justice and peace. To know shalom requires the achievement of *both* justice *and* peace. They are inseparable ingredients of the same reality.

On the one hand, there can be no peace without justice.

Then justice will dwell in the wilderness,
and righteousness abide in the fruitful field.
The effect of righteousness will be peace,
and the result of righteousness, quietness and trust
forever (Isaiah 32:16-18).

I will appoint Peace as your overseer
and Righteousness as your taskmaster.
Violence shall no more be heard in your land,
devastation or destruction within your borders;
you shall call your walls Salvation,
and your gates Praise. . . (Isaiah 60:17-19).

On the other hand, justice cannot ultimately be established by nonpeaceful means. There is no justice in war. "They do not know how to do right," fumes Amos, "those who store up violence and robbery in their strongholds" (3:10, see also Amos 1:3-2:4 and Isaiah 10:5-19). That justice requires peacemaking is made crystal clear in a passage from Isaiah 42 which, as we will see, seems to have been central to Jesus' sense of mission.

Here is my servant, whom I uphold,
my chosen, in whom my soul delights;
I have put my spirit upon him;
he will bring forth justice to the nations.
He will not cry or lift up his voice,
or make it heard in the street;
a bruised reed he will not break,
and a dimly burning wick he will not quench;
he will faithfully bring forth justice.
He will not grow faint or be crushed
until he has established justice in the earth. . .
(42:1-7; compare with Isaiah 61:1-11).

- *Covenant*
  Covenant is the Bible's word for committed relationship or, more accurately, for the formal commitment which brings the relationship into existence and specifies the rights and responsibilities of both parties. At the heart of the biblical story is the covenant made between God and Israel. In an act of undeserved grace, God chooses to enter into a unique relationship with Israel, a relationship that is ultimately intended for the benefit of all other nations as well.

  The conditions of this covenant relationship are spelled out in the Torah, the law given to Moses on Mount Sinai and gradually unfolded and developed through succeeding generations. This law reveals what is needed for Israel to live in shalom, to experience what the creator God always intended for the human community. The law derives its authority not from the coercive power of the state, but from the will and purpose of God for human blessing and fulfillment. Peace and justice will result if Israel remains loyal to its relationship with God by living according to God's law. Among other things, this law requires all covenant members to act with justice and mercy towards each other.

Biblical justice is therefore covenant justice. It is the practical outworking of Israel's special relationship with God. Justice flows from a life of obedience to the law of God, a law that derives its character from a larger vision of shalom, of God's intentions for human life. Law, justice, and covenant are thus overlapping or interpenetrating concepts in the Bible.

• *Torah*

Law, by definition, involves legislation. The same is true of biblical law; it contains hundreds of legal requirements and rulings. But biblical law is not legislation in the modern sense. Modern law codes are impersonal, technically precise, comprehensive, and self-consistent. Language is used literally in order to eliminate or minimize ambiguity. The primary audience of modern legislation is the professional legal establishment that must interpret and enforce its provisions.

Biblical law by comparison has a more pronounced pedagogical or educational function. It is addressed not just to legal specialists but to the entire community, spelling out in simple terms what life in covenant relationship with God entails (see especially Deuteronomy 29:10-12). Torah really means "instruction"; it is God's means of instruction in righteousness. Hence, the lyrical delight of the psalmist:

> The law of the LORD is perfect, reviving the soul;
> the decrees of the LORD are sure,
>   making wise the simple;
> the precepts of the LORD are right,
>   rejoicing the heart;

the commandment of the LORD is clear,
  enlightening the eyes;
the fear of the LORD is pure, enduring forever;
the ordinances of the LORD are true and righteous
  altogether.
More to be desired are they than gold,
  even much fine gold; sweeter also than honey
  and drippings of the honeycomb (19:7-10).

The fundamental tenets of covenant law are catalogued in the Decalogue or Ten Commandments, which fix the outer limits of behavior consistent with covenant membership: no idolatry, no murder, no stealing, no adultery, no greed, and so on (Exodus 20:1-17; Deuteronomy 5:6-21). These core principles are then translated elsewhere into concrete social legislation, partly in the form of general edicts or statutes that prohibit or enjoin certain actions in general, and partly in the form of particular case laws that address the specifics of individual situations.

In neither case are we dealing with hard and fast regulations that had to be applied to the letter in every situation. The array of diverse stipulations that make up the Mosaic Torah are better understood as representative samples of legal reasoning, built up steadily over time and in widely different circumstances, from which guidance could be drawn for other situations. In drawing such guidance, judges had considerable discretion. They were guided by the written Torah but also by precedent, circumstance, and oral tradition. The imperative was to "do justice and only justice," not simply to enforce positive legislation (Deuteronomy 16:18-20; 17:8-13).

All this may help explain what, to modern minds, is one of the most disturbing features of Old Testament law: its frequent recourse to capital punishment. About 20 offenses carry the death penalty. This is much less than the several hundred capital crimes in eighteenth-century European law, but still a lot. Even such "trivial" wrongs as striking a parent or committing adultery, having sex with someone else's fiancé, or breaching Sabbath rules are punishable by death. One might presume the streets of ancient Israel ran knee-deep in blood.

But there is good reason to doubt that in such cases the prescribed penalties were meant to be implemented literally. There are too many stories in the Old Testament in which people guilty of capital offenses are not executed to think that the penalties were applied rigidly. The purpose of attaching the ultimate sanction to certain behaviors was to mark them as especially serious. The judicial death threat was intended to get people's attention, to issue a solemn warning against the destructive consequences of particular misdeeds, especially those that breach the central covenantal principles articulated in the Ten Commandments. (Violations of seven of the Ten Commandments carry the death penalty in biblical legislation.) So the fact that biblical law declares that certain deeds are so serious as to be worthy of death is *not* to say that death was invariably, or even typically, exacted for actual offending.

- *Deed-Consequence*

This leads us to the difficult question of the place of divine punishment in the biblical understanding of justice. As we will see later, there is much said in the Bible about God's punishment of sinners, both of individual wrongdoers and of the nation as a whole for its disobedience and unfaithfulness. Sometimes the threat of punishment is used to dissuade people from persisting in sin and rebellion. At other times, the natural and military disasters that befall the nation are depicted as God's punishment of Israel for its failure to maintain the covenant relationship. Human calamities, in other words, are interpreted as visitations of divine wrath (see Romans 1:18-32). What are we to make of this way of viewing individual distress and historical disaster?

Biblical assertions about God's active, punitive intervention in human affairs need to be assessed in light of the basic worldview conviction that deeds carry their own inherent outcomes. There are forces at work within human actions themselves that carry the doers along in their wakes, bringing either blessing or bane, depending on whether the deeds are good or bad. (The classic text is Deuteronomy 30.) There is a Sin-Disaster connection on the one hand and a Righteousness-Blessing connection on the other. "Misfortune pursues sinners, but prosperity rewards the righteous"(Proverbs 13:21). This helps explain why a whole series of Hebrew terms are used to describe both an action and its consequences. The word *hatta't*, for example, means both "sin" and "disaster" and is perhaps the closest Hebrew word for "punishment."

This deed-consequence construct is not thought of as some kind of impersonal cause-and-effect mechanism that works independently of God. On the contrary, God is the one who ensures that the process operates in the first place. God is intimately involved in the interplay between human actions and their consequences. But while God's direct agency in meting out punishment (or blessing) is repeatedly affirmed by the biblical writers, there remains an important sense in which people reap what they themselves, or others, have sown by their actions. The punishment is often, in reality, self-inflicted.

God is responsible inasmuch as God actively ensures that human beings inherit the legacy of their deeds. As the apostle Paul puts it, God "gives people up" to their choices (Romans 1:24, 26, 28).

Understood this way, even judicial punishments imposed by human courts may be viewed within a biblical perspective as an expression of God's wrath (see, for example, Romans 13:3-6). This is not to suggest that God necessarily authorizes or administers individual punishments. Rather, the punishments relate to God's wrath in the sense that the just imposition of legal penalties for wrongdoing serves to dramatize or externalize a deep moral truth grounded in the way God has made reality: Human actions are of consequential importance, and we cannot escape responsibility for those consequences, for this is an essential prerequisite for human freedom.

- *Atonement-Forgiveness*

A brief word needs to be said, finally, about the mechanisms for dealing with sin in the Bible. Modern readers sometimes assume that because the atonement rituals of the Old Testament involve the sacrifice of animals or the use of scapegoats, the whole system depended on vicarious punishment (see Leviticus 4-5, 8-9, 16; compare with Exodus 29, Numbers 19, Deuteronomy 21, Hebrews 9-10). In this view, sacrifice was the means by which God could redirect judgment away from sinful people onto an innocent victim, thereby clearing the way to confer forgiveness on sinners without compromising the demands of justice. This scheme is then used to explain how in the New Testament the atoning death of Christ achieves salvation.

But this is an unlikely explanation for atonement practices in the Bible. In the biblical worldview, sin is considered to be not only a matter of moral failure incurring guilt, but also a source of pollution or contamination which threatens to spread like an infectious disease unless it is eliminated. In this respect, the sin-offering functions as a means of vicarious *cleansing*, not vicarious punishment. The sacrificial animal serves to represent those who offer it. By laying their hands on the animal, the offerers symbolically transfer their sinful identity to their representative so that it can be expunged. Forgiveness results for them.

But this forgiveness is not granted because substitutionary punishment has occurred, but because the people have exhibited remorse and dedication through their participation in the ritual. The covenant relationship, broken by the people's sin, is thus restored, and it is this restoration, not some act of vicarious punishment, that turns away God's wrath and satisfies God's justice. Things have been made right again. In the New Testament, of course, it is Jesus' representative sacrificial death that serves as God's definitive means of "right-making" for human sinfulness and impurity.

Summary

Biblical reflection on justice takes place within a theological and cultural worldview that is, in many ways, quite different from ours. According to this worldview, Israel exists in unique *covenant* relationship with God. This relationship depends on God's *justice*, God's absolute goodness and faithfulness to commitments. Israel upholds the covenant by living in accordance with God's law, the *Torah*. The purpose of this law is to enable Israel to experience *shalom*, that state of well-being and wholeness that God always intended for humankind in creation. Such shalom, however, is constantly disrupted by Israel's sinful *deeds*, which bring their own dire consequences. God's law provides a means of diverting these *consequences* onto a sin-offering, so that *atonement* can be made and *forgiveness* experienced.

The biblical concept of justice derives its distinctive contours from this complex of interrelated convictions. It is time now to look more closely at these justice contours.

3.
The Contours of Biblical Justice

We are now in a position to identify some of the particular emphases and insights that give biblical teaching on justice its distinctive shape. The place to begin is where justice itself begins, in the nature of God.

An Attribute of God

The biblical writers consider justice to be, before all else, a personal quality or virtue of God. This explains the enormous concern they have for the subject. Justice belongs to the very being of God. Justice is not something God aspires to; it is the heart of who God is and what God does (Isaiah 24:16, 30:18, 45:21; Genesis 18:25, 2 Chronicles 12:6; Nehemiah 9:8; Psalm 7:9, 89:14, 97:2, 103:17; Jeremiah 9:24; Daniel 9:14; Zephaniah 3:5; Zechariah 8:8; Romans 3:26, 9:14; 1 Peter 2:23; Revelation 15:3).

> I will proclaim the name of the LORD;
> ascribe greatness to our God!
> The Rock, his work is perfect, and all his ways are just.
> A faithful God, without deceit, just and upright is he
> (Deuteronomy 32:3-4).

> The LORD is just in all his ways,
> and kind in all his doings (Psalm 145:17).

The Contours of Biblical Justice

As an attribute of the Creator God, justice furnishes the ground plan of creation. It is, according to the psalmist, the "foundation" of God's throne, the fundamental ground of the cosmos (Psalm 89:14, 97:2; compare with Psalm 102:25; Job 38:4; Isaiah 48:13). Justice designates the "right ordering" of the universe, the way God intends reality to operate. God has created the world in a manner that expresses and depends upon God's own inherent justice and righteousness.

It is this basic conviction—that God is the source and measure of all justice—that permits the biblical writers to condemn injustice wherever they find it. It compels them to announce God's judgment on the evil deeds of all nations, not just Israel. All nations are answerable to God, for God "will judge the *world* with righteousness, and the *peoples* with equity" (Habakkuk 1:13; compare with Malachi 2:17).

> **Justice is the heart of who God is and what God does.**

This universal reach of divine justice is strikingly pictured in Psalm 82. The psalmist imagines an international courtroom setting where Yahweh, the God of Israel, accuses the gods or rulers of other nations of perverting justice in their respective realms. The psalm ends by underscoring the accountability of all peoples to God's justice.

> God has taken his place in the divine council; in the midst of the gods he holds judgment: "How long will you judge unjustly and show partiality to the wicked? Give justice to the weak and the orphan; maintain the right of the lowly and the destitute. Rescue the weak and the needy; deliver them from the hand of the wicked." . . . Rise up, O God, judge the earth; for all the nations belong to you! (Psalm 82:1-4, 8)

It is such unwavering belief in the inherent justice of God that gives rise to the painful problem of *theodicy* (literally "the justification of God"). How can the goodness and justice of God be vindicated in light of obvious evil? How can the all-powerful Creator God, the Deity who "loves justice," tolerate such brutal injustices in the world? (Isaiah 61:8; Psalm 33:5, 37:28, 99:4) The prophet Habakkuk puts the problem eloquently:

> Your eyes are too pure to behold evil,
> and you cannot look on wrongdoing.
> Why do you look on the treacherous,
> and are silent when the wicked
> swallow those more righteous than they?
> (Psalm 98:9; compare with 9:8, 96:10,13, 97:1-2, 6,
> 99:1-4; Romans 1:18, 3:6)

Note here that the prophet does not dispute the reality of God's own justice and integrity, despite the apparent triumph of evil in everyday affairs. Whatever the contradictions of present experience, the biblical writers never toy with the possibility that God's personal justice might somehow be flawed or God's power limited. For them, there can be no doubting that Yahweh is perfect in justice, for Israel had witnessed the triumph of God's justice in her own history (Deuteronomy 32:4; 2 Samuel 22:31; Psalm 18:30). She had seen God intervene to liberate her from the oppression of slavery, to lead her safely through the wilderness, and to constitute her as a free, independent people. Israel's own concrete experience had proved forever that "Yahweh is a God of justice" (Isaiah 30:18).

Yahweh's justice was also confirmed in the gift of the law to Israel. In this law, God requires the covenant people to act towards one another in the same way God has acted towards them—with justice, mercy, and equity.

You shall not deprive a resident alien or an orphan of justice; you shall not take a widow's garment in pledge. Remember that you were a slave in Egypt and the LORD your God redeemed you from there; therefore I command you to do this (Deuteronomy 24:17-18; compare with Exodus 20:2ff; Leviticus 19:36, 25:38, 26:13; Numbers 15:41; Deuteronomy 5:6ff).

So for the biblical authors, justice is rooted in God's very being and determines all God's interactions with the world. When the great American civil rights leader Martin Luther King, Jr. declared "the universe is on the side of justice," he was echoing a fundamental presupposition of the biblical tradition. Justice is the objective foundation of all reality. This justice is known, not primarily through philosophical speculation, but through observing God's *actions* to liberate the oppressed, and through heeding God's *word* in the Law and the Prophets to protect and care for the weak.

> Our knowledge of justice springs ultimately from our knowledge of God.

This means that our knowledge of justice springs ultimately from our knowledge of God, and that there can be no true knowledge of God without an appreciation of God's own unfailing dedication to justice.

An Emulation of God

In the biblical creation narratives, it is only human beings who are made in the image and likeness of God (Genesis 1:26-27; compare with 2:7, 5:1-2, 9:6). Humans are created to be representatives of God—a kind of icon of God in the world. They are the means by which God's loving rule is to be made visible on earth. Since God is a God of jus-

> **Those who bear God's image must also be agents of justice.**

tice, those who bear God's image must also be agents of justice. They are to learn from God what justice means and to reproduce what they learn in all their activities in the world.

Tragically, the entry of sin has distorted humanity's capacity to know the truth about God and to live justly. Rivalry, violence, and corruption have erupted in the human community (Genesis 4:1-16, 23-24, 6:1-8, 11-13). But God's redemptive activity, beginning with the call of Abraham and the election of Israel, is aimed at reinstalling humankind to its intended role in creation. In God's saving activity toward Israel, the nature of divine justice is disclosed afresh, and, once again, its beneficiaries are instructed to replicate what they have seen (Leviticus 11:45, 19:2, 20:26; Numbers 15:40; 1 Peter 1:16).

> O my people . . . I brought you up from the land of Egypt, and redeemed you from the house of slavery; and I sent before you Moses, Aaron, and Miriam. O my people, remember . . . the saving acts of the LORD. . . . He has told you, O mortal, what is good; and what does the LORD require of you but to do justice, and to love kindness, and to walk humbly with your God? (Micah 6:3-8)

> For the LORD your God is God of gods and Lord of lords, the great God, mighty and awesome, who is not partial and takes no bribe, who executes justice for the orphan and the widow, and who loves the strangers, providing them food and clothing. You shall also love

the stranger, for you were strangers in the land of Egypt (Deuteronomy 10:17-19).

Emulating God's justice is, according to the biblical prophets, the evidence of what it means to know God. True knowledge of God entails both an appreciation of God's own unswerving devotion to justice and a commitment to live one's personal life in conformity to God's justice (see Hosea 4:1-2, 5:4, 6:6; Jeremiah 2:8, 4:22, 9:2-6, 24, 22:16; Isaiah 58:2. Also Titus 1:16; 1 John 4:8). Knowing God, as Jeremiah affirms, is much more important than possessing wealth or education or power. But there is more to knowing God than confessing dogmas or having religious experiences. It involves discovering God's personal passions and priorities and responding to them in like manner.

Thus says the LORD: Do not let the wise boast in their wisdom, do not let the mighty boast in their might, do not let the wealthy boast in their wealth; but let those who boast boast in this, that they understand and know me, that I am the LORD; I act with steadfast love, justice, and righteousness in the earth, for in these things I delight, says the LORD (Jeremiah 9:23-24; compare with 1 Corinthians 1:18-21).

Elsewhere Jeremiah attacks King Jehoiakim for building an ostentatious palace on the back of exploited labor. He calls on the king to copy the commitment of his father Josiah, "doing justice and righteousness," which not only brought blessing on Josiah but demonstrated his true understanding of God.

Woe to him who builds his house by unrighteousness, and his upper rooms by injustice; who makes his neighbors work for nothing, and does not give them their wages; who says, "I will build myself a spacious house with large upper rooms," and who cuts out windows for it, paneling it with cedar, and painting it with vermilion. Are you a king because you compete in cedar? Did not your father eat and drink and do justice and righteousness? Then it was well with him. He judged the cause of the poor and needy; then it was well. Is not this to know me? says the LORD (Jeremiah 22:13-16).

An Object of Hope

Biblical hope—that confident expectation of a better future—is rooted in the knowledge of God's justice and faithfulness. Because God is the source and champion of justice, and because God is utterly reliable, there is *always* hope for positive change. The present may be blighted by evil and injustice, but the "God of hope," who is forever on the side of the oppressed, is moving history mysteriously in the direction of final deliverance (Romans 15:13, 8:18-30). "Happy are those whose help is in the God of Jacob," the psalmist exclaims, "whose *hope* is in the Lord their God . . . who *executes* justice for the oppressed" (Psalm 146:5-7; compare with 10:17-18, 103:6-7).

The meaning of justice, we have seen, may be learned by observing God's actions in the past and present. But the full revelation of justice remains an object of hope. It is something yet to be witnessed. This has two important implications for how we are to view current circumstances.

- *Grounds for criticism:* It means that no existing political system or economic order can ever be regarded as the full, or even as an adequate, realization of justice. All human social structures and centers of power are denied ultimate significance. Every human attempt to create justice, when measured against the perfect justice of God's coming kingdom, is inescapably partial and limited. There is, therefore, always room for criticism; there is never ground for complacency; there is always need for improvement.

- *A call to action:* Present injustices must never simply be tolerated or accepted as inevitable. We are not meant to resign ourselves to the evils of the world, while waiting passively for God's coming to sweep them away. Instead, we are to work tirelessly in partnership with God for the greater attainment of justice here and now, knowing that God shall ultimately bring our efforts to fruition in the renewal of creation. God's coming justice is the culmination of, not a substitute for, human striving for greater justice here and now.

A Primary Obligation

The pursuit of justice must be a primary obligation of the people of God.

Justice is always an effort. It doesn't just happen. It doesn't spontaneously spring into existence. Nor is it the automatic or accidental by-product of something else, such as the operation of market forces or the spread of Western democracy. Justice requires commitment and struggle. Like peace, it has to be pursued with dedication, for there are powerful forces at work in every society with vested interest in maintaining structures of exploitation and oppression (Isaiah 51:1; 1 Timothy 6:11; 2 Timothy 2:2; compare with Psalm 34:14; Romans 14:19; Hebrews 12:14; 1 Peter 3:11; 1 Corinthians 14:1). The Preacher in Ecclesiastes knows this all too well.

Again I saw all the oppressions that are practiced under the sun. Look, the tears of the oppressed—with no one to comfort them! On the side of their oppressors there was power—with no one to comfort them (Ecclesiastes 4:1).

If you see in a province the oppression of the poor and the violation of justice and right, do not be amazed at the matter; for the high official is watched by a higher, and there are yet higher ones over them (Ecclesiastes 5:8).

The pursuit of justice must therefore be a primary obligation of the people of God. It is so critical, say the biblical prophets, that without a commitment to justice, all other means of worshipping God, even those commanded by God's law, are bankrupt. In the absence of justice, Amos declares, religious performances merely nauseate God.

I hate, I despise your festivals, and I take no delight in your solemn assemblies. Even though you offer me your burnt offerings and grain offerings, I will not accept them; and the offerings of well-being of your fatted animals I will not look upon. Take away from me the noise of your songs; I will not listen to the melody of your harps. But let justice roll down like waters, and righteousness like an ever flowing stream (Amos 5:21-24).

Micah warns that even multiplying the quantity and quality of sacrificial offerings cannot offset the want of justice, kindness, and humility.

With what shall I come before the LORD, and bow myself before God on high? Shall I come before him with burnt offerings, with calves a year old? Will the LORD be pleased with thousands of rams, with ten thousand rivers of oil? Shall I give my firstborn for my transgressions, the fruit of my body for the sin of my soul? He has told you, O mortal, what is good; and what does the LORD require of you but to do justice, to love kindness, and to walk humbly with your God? (Micah 6:6-8)

Isaiah, too, accents God's weariness with religious activities that mask injustice and oppression. God refuses, as a matter principle, to listen to those who pray with blood on their hands.

When you stretch out your hands, I will hide my eyes from you; even though you make many prayers, I will not listen; your hands are full of blood. Wash yourselves; make yourselves clean; remove the evil of your doings from before my eyes; cease to do evil, learn to do good; seek justice, rescue the oppressed, defend the orphan, plead for the widow (Isaiah 1:12-17).

Elsewhere Isaiah denounces the use of religious fasting as an effectual means of "seeking God," "delighting in God," "drawing near" to God, and "calling on God" when a nation fails to practice justice. Fasting has no leverage on God when workers are oppressed, violence is perpetrated, and the poor go hungry.

Is not this the fast that I choose: to loose the bonds of injustice, to undo the thongs of the yoke, to let the oppressed go free, and to break every yoke? Is it not to share your bread with the hungry, and bring the homeless poor into your house; when you see the naked, to cover them, and not to hide yourself from your own kin? . . . Then you shall call, and the LORD will answer; you shall cry for help, and he will say, "Here I am" (Isaiah 58:1-14).

For the biblical prophets, then, holiness is not simply a case of ethnic distinction, of being separated from other nations as God's chosen people (Deuteronomy 7:6, 14:2-21, 26:19; compare with Leviticus 20:26). Nor is it primarily a matter of observing prescribed religious rituals. *The essential mark of holiness is a lifestyle of justice.* Just as "the LORD of hosts is exalted by justice, and the Holy God shows himself holy by righteousness", so, too, God's people are to reveal their set-apartness by their passion for justice (Isaiah 5:16). For holiness means wholeness as well as separation. It describes a life of completeness and unity and goodness, a life that reflects God's own integrity and self-consistency, a life that is animated by justice.

A Commitment to Action

Several times we have stressed that justice in the Bible is not an abstract philosophical idea or a mathematical principle of evaluation. It is a description of what God is like and of how God relates to the world (Psalm 103:13-14, 145:9). It is shown most clearly in the way God has acted towards oppressed Israel, and to the oppressed within Israel (Exodus 3:7-8; Psalm 10:13-17, 35:10, 140:12; Jeremiah 20:13). Justice is not a static ideal; it is not the maintenance of some steady state in society. The accent in biblical justice falls on positive action, the exercising of power to resist the oppressor and set the oppressed free. This is why Amos pictures justice as a thundering river rather than, as in the Western tradition, a neatly balanced set of scales (Amos 5:21-24).

There is more to biblical justice than the preservation of law and order.

There is more to biblical justice than the preservation of law and order. For laws can be unjust and order may depend on violence. Biblical justice requires an activist response to systemic evil, a radical intervention to "loose the bonds of injustice, to undo the thongs of the yoke, to let the oppressed go free, and to break every yoke" (Isaiah 58:6). It entails a steadfast commitment to "execute justice in the morning, and deliver from the hand of the oppressor anyone who has been robbed" (Jeremiah 21:12).

According to Isaiah, God is outraged not only at the existence of injustice, but at the failure of anyone to do anything about it.

> For our transgressions before you are many, and our sins testify against us . . . Justice is turned back, and righteousness stands at a distance; for truth stumbles in the public square, and uprightness cannot enter. Truth is lacking, and whoever turns from evil is despoiled. The LORD saw it, and it displeased him that there was no justice. He saw that there was no one, and was appalled that there was no one to intervene; so his own arm brought him victory, and his righteousness upheld him. He put on righteousness like a breastplate, and a helmet of salvation on his head; he put on garments of vengeance for clothing, and wrapped himself in fury as in a mantle (Isaiah 59:12-17; compare with Ezekiel 22:25-30).

Of course it is those who possess authority in society who are most responsible for the pursuit of justice. What is almost universally accepted in political theory is true of the Bible as well—securing justice is the first and foremost task of government. Moses instructed tribal leaders and officials in Israel to administer "justice and only justice."

You shall appoint judges and officials throughout your tribes, in all your towns that the LORD your God is giving you, and they shall render just decisions for the people. You must not distort justice; you must not show partiality; and you must not accept bribes, for a bribe blinds the eyes of the wise and subverts the cause of those who are in the right. Justice, and only justice, you shall pursue, so that you may live and occupy the land that the LORD your God is giving you (Deuteronomy 16:18-20; compare with Exodus 18:13-23).

The primary responsibility of the Hebrew king was similarly to ensure that justice prevailed in the land by restraining the strong and defending the weak.

Because the LORD loved Israel forever,
he has made you king to execute justice
    and righteousness (1 Kings 10:9; compare with
    2 Samuel 8:15; Deuteronomy 17:18-20).

Give the king your justice, O God,
and your righteousness to a king's son.
May he judge your people with righteousness,
and your poor with justice (Psalm 72:1-2).

Hear the word of the LORD, O King of Judah, sitting on the throne of David—you, and your servants, and your people who enter these gates. Thus says the LORD: Act with justice and righteousness, and deliver from the hand of the oppressor anyone who has been robbed. And do no wrong or violence to the alien, the orphan, and the widow, or shed innocent blood in this place (Jeremiah 22:2-3, 15-16; compare with Ezekiel 45:9).

Since executing justice was the highest royal duty, it is not surprising that the task of the future Messiah—the coming ideal king—was to bring the fullness of God's justice and peace to earth.

Behold the days are coming, says the Lord, when I will raise up for David a righteous Branch, and he shall reign as king and deal wisely, and shall execute justice and righteousness in the land (Jeremiah 23:5).

His authority shall grow continually, and there shall be endless peace for the throne of David and his kingdom. He will establish and uphold it with justice and with righteousness from this time onward and forevermore. The zeal of the LORD of hosts will do this (Isaiah 9:2-7; compare with 11:1-5, 42:1-4; 61:1-9).

In the New Testament, as we will see in the next chapter, Jesus is the one who fulfills this expectation. He is God's chosen servant to "bring justice to victory" (Matthew 12:18-23; compare with Isaiah 42:1-4; Matthew 23:23).

A Relational Reality

If justice is a personal attribute of God, and if human beings as God's image-bearers are called to emulate God's justice in the way they live with one another in community, it follows that *justice is all about relationships*. It has to do with God's relationship with humanity and the world, and with the relationship of human beings to each other and to the larger created order.

> Biblical justice is all about relationships.

This, in fact, is one of the most distinctive features of biblical teaching on justice and righteousness. Biblical justice is comprehensively relational. It is not a private attribute that an individual has on his or her own, independent of anyone else. Nor is it a set of abstract norms about balance or equity or fairness. Justice means doing all that is necessary to create and sustain healthy, constant, and life-giving relationships between persons. Justice is to be measured by the extent to which people honor their obligation to live in relationships that uphold the equal dignity and rights of the other. Both elements are important—relationships that are wholesome, and faithfulness to the demands of such relationships by all parties involved.

This is often what the biblical writers have in mind when they speak of God's justice or righteousness. God is just because God remains loyal to the covenant relationship with Israel, even when Israel proves faithless to this relationship. God's justice means God can be counted on, no matter what the covenant partner does. Perhaps the clearest affirmation that God's justice consists of God's faithfulness to relationship is found in Romans 3.

> Then what advantage has the Jew? Or what is the value of circumcision? Much, in every way. For in the first place the Jews were entrusted with the oracles of God. What if some were unfaithful? Will their faithlessness nullify the faithfulness of God? By no means! Although everyone is a liar, let God be proved true, as it is written, "So that you may be justified in your words, and prevail in your judging." But if our injustice serves to confirm the justice of God, what should we say? That God is unjust to inflict wrath on us? (I speak in a human way.) By no means! For then how could God judge the world?

Here the apostle Paul affirms that God's justice towards Israel—that is, God's undying commitment to covenant relationship with the chosen people—is not cancelled out by Israel's injustice; that is, by her failure to remain true to God by living justly in accordance with God's law. Yet, Paul explains, God's commitment to Israel does not mean that God can simply ignore her failure or wink at her sin. Were God to turn a blind eye to Israel's injustice, God would no longer be fit to judge the world with impartial justice (Romans 2:1-3:20). God must deal with Israel's failure without failing to remain absolutely committed to Israel—which, for Paul, is what the death of Jesus is all about.

The relational character of biblical justice helps to explain why the biblical writers see no tension between justice and mercy. God's mercy is indeed an expression of God's justice.

> Therefore the LORD waits to be gracious to you; therefore he will rise up to show mercy to you. For the LORD is a God of justice; blessed are all those who wait for him (Isaiah 30:18; compare with Psalm 85:10).

We often think of mercy and justice as opposites. To show mercy when wrongdoing has occurred means suspending or disregarding the penalty which justice requires. Mercy thus represents a kind of injustice. But this is only the case if we think of justice in strictly arithmetical or legalistic terms. If instead we understand justice in terms of restoring healthy relationships, then mercy is often the best way to get there. Mercy helps to bring about, rather than to interfere with, justice. Compassionate acceptance of human fallibility is essential to the functioning of healthy relationships. Where failure occurs, justice must be seasoned with mercy, or it is not true justice.

There is no tension between justice and mercy.

> Thus says the LORD of hosts: Render true judgments, show kindness and mercy to one another (Zechariah 7:9; compare with Hosea 12:6; Micah 6:8; James 2:13).

A Partiality for the Disadvantaged

We come now to one of the most important insights of biblical teaching on justice: it requires different priorities in different settings. In some circumstances justice requires a disinterested impartiality, a repudiation of all favoritism. In other circumstances it demands an unequivocal partiality, a definite bias towards the interests of certain parties over those of others. Justice is both impartial and partial, biased and unbiased, equal and unequal, depending on the issues at stake.

> *Sometimes justice requires impartiality, at other times partiality.*

On the one hand, biblical law considers *impartiality* to be critically important when dealing with *criminal wrongdoing or in arbitrating disputes between litigants.* Unlike other ancient societies, where different laws and different penalties applied to different classes, Israelite criminal and procedural law was radically egalitarian. All members of the community were subject to the same standards, and judges were explicitly required to disregard social and economic status in hearing cases and to refrain from selling justice to the highest bidder.

Give the members of your community a fair hearing, and judge rightly between one person and another, whether citizen or resident alien. You must not be partial in judging: hear out the small and the great alike; you shall not be intimidated by anyone, for the judgment is God's. Any case that is too hard for you, bring to me, and I will hear it (Deuteronomy 1:16-17).

You must not distort justice; you must not show partiality; and you must not accept bribes, for a bribe blinds the eyes of the wise and subverts the cause of those who are in the right (Deuteronomy 16:19; compared with Micah 7:3-4; Amos 5:12).

Such procedural fairness is justified, once again, by an appeal to the equity of God's justice, "for there is no perversion of justice with the LORD our God, or partiality, or taking of bribes" (2 Chronicles 19:7; compare with Deuteronomy 10:17; Acts 10:34; Romans 2:11; Colossians 3:25; Ephesians 6:9; 1 Peter 1:17).

While impartiality is essential in the Bible to the administration of procedural and retributive justice, a quite different emphasis emerges with respect to *social justice* (which deals with the way wealth, social resources, and political power are distributed in society). Here a definite *partiality* is to be exhibited. A special concern or bias is to be shown for the welfare of four groups in particular—widows, orphans, resident aliens (or immigrants), and the poor.

You shall not wrong or oppress a resident alien, for you were aliens in the land of Egypt. You shall not abuse any widow or orphan. If you do abuse them, when they cry out to me, I will surely heed their cry; my wrath will burn, and I will kill you with the sword, and your wives shall become widows and your children orphans (Exodus 22:21-24).

You shall not deprive a resident alien or an orphan of justice; you shall not take a widow's garment in pledge. Remember that you were a slave in Egypt and the LORD your God redeemed you from there; therefore I command you to do this (Deuteronomy 24:17-18; Exodus 23:9).

Ah, you who make iniquitous decrees, who write oppressive statutes, to turn aside the needy from justice
and to rob the poor of my people of their right, that widows may be your spoil, and that you may make the orphans your prey! What will you do on the day of punishment, in the calamity that will come from far away?
To whom will you flee for help, and where will you
leave your wealth? (Isaiah 10:1-4)

Thus says the LORD of hosts: Render true judgments,
show kindness and mercy to one another; do not oppress the widow, the orphan, the alien, or the poor; and
do not devise evil in your hearts against one another
(Zechariah 7:9-10).

Partiality for such groups (sometimes other parties are
also included, such as prisoners, the sick, and the broken-
hearted) is commended, yet again, by the nature of God's
justice, for "the LORD maintains the cause of the needy,
and executes justice for the poor" (Psalm 140:12; compare
with Proverbs 14:31, 22:2). At first sight, the idea of a pre-
sumed bias in favor of certain groups in society seems an-
tithetical to justice. Should not a just society aspire to treat
all people exactly the same, irrespective of wealth, nation-
ality, or family status? Not necessarily. There are two main
reasons why, in the biblical perspective, the struggle for social justice must be biased in favor of certain parties:

- *Because some groups in the community are more frequently the victims of injustice than other groups are.*
  God has created all people equal in worth and given to
  all equal rights of access to the abundance of creation
  (Psalm 8:5-7, 115:16; compare with 24:1). But individuals are also created different in gender, race, personali-
  ty, capacity, and gifting. Injustice occurs when these dif-

ferences are exploited in such a way that some are denied their God-given rights so that others can accumulate unneeded excess. What widows, orphans, migrants, and the poor have in common, especially in a patriarchal society, is their vulnerability to exploitation. The widow has no husband to watch over her rights, the orphan has no parents, the poor have no money, the stranger has no friends. Their rights are more easily trampled than are those of the rich and powerful—who still possess legitimate rights but usually have the means to protect those rights by themselves.

• *Because the condition of the impoverished and the oppressed violates God's intentions for the world.* The existence of grinding poverty is an evil. It is not God's will that some should live in splendor and opulence while others starve and die. It is not God's will that some should hoard food and surplus land, while others languish in debt and servitude (Numbers 11:31-33; Leviticus 25:8-17). This is why meeting the needs of the poor is not a matter of charity in the Bible, but an act of justice, for it helps move society in the direction God intends the world to be. In the biblical understanding, the litmus test for measuring the extent of justice in society is how its most vulnerable members are faring. The most salient indicator of injustice is where people are deprived access to the essential resources they need to survive and flourish as free and productive human beings.

God's bias or "preferential option" for the poor is, ultimately, in the interests of equity. In the perennial struggle for social justice, in which the scales seem always to be tipped on the side of the wealthy and powerful, God evens the balance by taking the side of the poor and defenseless. God is not a disinterested observer of the struggle; instead God "executes justice for the oppressed . . . gives food to the hungry ────────── . . . sets the prisoners free . . . opens the eyes

God evens the balance by taking the side of the poor and the defenseless.
──────────

of the blind . . . lifts up those who are bowed down . . . loves the righteous . . . watches over the strangers . . . upholds the orphan and the widow, but the way of the wicked he brings to ruin" (Psalm 146:5-9).

But precisely *how* does God defend the cause of the poor? How does God feed the hungry and show solidarity with the oppressed? How, for the biblical authors, is the bias of God's justice visible in practice? In several ways:

1. *Through God's historic intervention to rescue powerless, impoverished Israel* from servitude in Egypt and to feed her in the wilderness. God's "bias" to poor Israel in the past, recalled through annual celebrations like Passover, proved forever God's active bias toward the poor.

2. *Through the inclusion in God's law of specific welfare provisions and protections for the poor and vulnerable.* Numerous laws guarantee access to food, clothing, shelter, and rest, even to the most destitute. Those without land of their own are given rights of access to the land of others in order to meet their basic needs for survival.

> When you reap your harvest in your field and forget a sheaf in the field, you shall not go back to get it; it shall be left for the alien, the orphan, and the widow, so that the LORD your God may bless you in all your undertakings. When you beat your olive trees, do not strip what is left; it shall be for the alien, the orphan, and the widow. When you gather the grapes of your vineyard, do not glean

what is left; it shall be for the alien, the orphan, and the widow. Remember that you were a slave in the land of Egypt; therefore I am commanding you to do this (Deuteronomy 24:19-22; compare also 14:28, 23:24-25; Leviticus 19:9-10).

Every third year, a tenth of the harvest is to be set aside in storehouses for the poor and dispossessed (Deuteronomy 14:28-29). Even during sabbatical years, when the fields were to be left fallow, the poor retained the right to gather food from them.

For six years you shall sow your land and gather in its yield; but the seventh year you shall let it rest and lie fallow, so that the poor of your people may eat; and what they leave the wild animals may eat. You shall do the same with your vineyard, and with your olive orchard (Exodus 23:10-11).

Sabbath and Jubilee regulations require the remittance of debts, the release of slaves, and restoration of land to its original owners (Deuteronomy 15:1-11; Leviticus 25:8-17; Exodus 23:10-11). These laws recognize the need for regular political action to counteract the inherent tendency in all economic systems to concentrate wealth and power in the hands of the few at the expense of the many. Scholars doubt that these revolutionary provisions were ever fully honored in practice. But they always served as an uncomfortable reminder to Israel of God's partiality towards the plight of the dispossessed.

3. *Through God's raising up of prophets to confront the rich and powerful,* including the king himself, with God's demand for justice and with dire warnings of judgment should they fail in their duty to care for the weak.

The LORD enters into judgment with the elders and princes of his people: It is you who have devoured the vineyard; the spoil of the poor is in your houses. "What do you mean by crushing my people, by grinding the face of the poor?" says the Lord GOD of hosts (Isaiah 3:14-15; compare with Amos 2:6-7, 4:1-3, 5:10-13; Jeremiah 5:26-29; Malachi 3:5; Zechariah 7:9-14).

4. *Through God's promise to the poor of a new day coming,* in which the hungry will be fed, the sick will be healed, captives will be released, and suffering will be ended (Isaiah 35:3-7, 61:1-9; compare with Luke 4:18-19). This promise brings comfort for the present and hope for the future. For what God promises, God is always at work to bring to pass.

> This God—his way is perfect;
> the promise of the LORD proves true;
> he is a shield for all who take refuge in him
> (Psalm 18:30; compare with 2 Samuel 22:31).

A Restorative Activity

God's partiality for the poor, we have suggested, is because of their greater vulnerability to unjust victimization. But the poor are not automatically virtuous. They are not always innocent of wrongdoing themselves. Where accusations are brought against them in court, biblical law requires the judicial system to treat all parties impartially.

> You shall not render an unjust judgment; you shall not be partial to the poor or defer to the great: with justice you shall judge your neighbor (Leviticus 19:15).

You shall not follow a majority in wrongdoing; when you bear witness in a lawsuit, you shall not side with the majority so as to pervert justice; nor shall you be partial to the poor in a lawsuit (Exodus 23:2-3).

But impartiality is essential only for establishing guilt or culpability. Once that has been decided, the fundamental goal of the biblical judicial system is to restore what has been damaged by the offending. Restoration is required at several levels—restoration of the victim to wholeness, restoration of the offender to a right standing in the community, and restoration of the wider society to peace and freedom from fear, sin, and pollution.

Punishment is not what satisfies the demands of justice.

Punishments are often prescribed for particular offenses in biblical legislation. But punishment is a means to an end, not an end in itself. Contrary to what many people think today, punishment as such is not what satisfies the demands of justice. Justice is satisfied by repentance, restoration, and renewal. Punishment serves as a mechanism for helping to promote such restoration.

For many crimes, the typical penalty was restitution to the victim plus compensation. Specific acts of restitution are prescribed in biblical law, based broadly on equivalence of value (Exodus 21:26-36). Some offenses demanded double restitution, or more, according to the seriousness of the offense and the attitude of the offender (Exodus 22:1, 4, 9; Proverbs 6:30-31; Exodus 22:7). If remorseful, the thief restored what was stolen plus a fifth (Leviticus 6:5). If the thief was caught with the goods on him he restored double. If he had already disposed of the goods and tried to conceal the offense, he had to restore four- or fivefold. If the thief could not pay, he might be taken as a slave by the injured party until he had worked off the debt (Exodus

22:3). But enslavement could only last for a maximum of six years or until the year of Jubilee (Exodus 21:1-6; Deuteronomy 15:12-17; Leviticus 25:39-55). Slavery was not as ghastly in the ancient Orient as in modern times; in fact, it could be argued that Hebrew slavery was a more humane institution than its modern equivalent of imprisonment.

Even in the case of punishments that appear to hurt the offender more than restore the victim, a larger restorative intention can be discerned. Punishments served an educative, more than a retributive, function in several ways:

- They helped the wider community to *recognize* those kinds of behaviors that constituted the most serious threats to its moral and spiritual well-being. The varying severity of punishments in biblical law reflects an underlying scale of values. Unlike other ancient societies, and all European societies up to the 18th century, biblical legislation never prescribes the death penalty for crimes against property. It is only specified for crimes against people and for violations of those central obligations of Israel's unique relationship with God. Only in rare cases was it mandatory to carry out the death penalty (Deuteronomy 13:8-9, 19:13, 21, 25:12; Numbers 35:31-34; compare with Genesis 4:11-15; Exodus 2:11-14, 2 Samuel 12:13, 14:11). As we saw in the previous chapter, the purpose of attaching such severe punishment to certain offenses was to mark the sinful and especially damaging nature of deeds that disregard human dignity and that deny Israel's vocation to be different from other nations.

- Punishments also *dramatized* the way in which evil deeds invariably carry destructive consequences, consequences that cannot be ignored but must be addressed. The best way to deal with these consequences is by repentance, atonement, forgiveness, and repair. Punishment helped evoke such repentance by spelling out, in unmistakable terms, the negative energy that had been released by the wrongful deeds.

Have I any pleasure in the death of the wicked, says the Lord GOD, and not rather that they should turn from their ways and live? (Ezekiel 18:23; compare with 2 Thessalonians 3:13-15; 1 Corinthians 5:5; 2 Corinthians 2:6-8; 1 Timothy 1:19-20; Hebrews 12:7-11)

In some cases, atonement or "purging evil from Israel," required the death of the offender, who was considered the source of a serious pollution which threatened the holiness and very existence of God's people (Numbers 35:33; compare with Deuteronomy 13:5-11, 16, 17:7, 12, 19:19, 21:21, 22:21-22, 24, 24:7; Leviticus 24:14; Judges 20:13; 2 Samuel 4:11). Even here, the punishment enabled the community to be restored to integrity.

- Punishments also served to *deter* copycat offending. If punishments demonstrate that certain behaviors are destructive to the community's welfare, those who witness them are thereby instructed to refrain from harming the well-being of themselves and of others.

If anyone secretly entices you ... saying, "Let us go worship other gods," whom neither you nor your ancestors have known ... stone them to death for trying to turn you away from the LORD your God, who brought you out of the land of Egypt, out of the house of slavery. Then all Israel shall hear and be afraid, and never again do any such wickedness (Deuteronomy

13:6-11; see also 17:12-13, 21:20-21; Acts 5:11; Romans 13:3-5, 1 Timothy 5:20).

Punishment, then, is an inescapable component of biblical jurisprudence. But the distinctive concern of biblical justice is not to punish sinners, but to restore shalom by clarifying and dealing with the damage caused by wrongdoing. Punishment was a tool for helping to achieve this.

Summary

Biblical justice is a complex, multi-faceted reality. It relates to every dimension of human experience, and it has many different applications. But arguably the term that best captures the spirit and direction of biblical justice, both social justice and criminal justice, is the word *restoration*. Justice flows from God's own being and designates the way God intends the world to be. But things have fallen into disorder; the shalom of creation has been ruptured. God responds by seeking to restore the world to the way it ought to be.

> God's justice is best characterized as restorative.

Biblical justice seeks to restore dignity and autonomy to those who have been unjustly deprived of access to sufficient resources in order to meet their own basic needs for physical survival and human fulfillment. God acts to reconstruct shalom by overthrowing oppressive powers and setting victims free, and by healing the destructive legacy of sin and death. To know this God is to learn about the meaning of justice. To love this God is to join in God's great campaign to restore justice to the world.

4.
Jesus and Justice

We have seen how the liberation of Israel from servitude in Egypt, and her establishment as an independent people, shows that God's justice is a liberating, community-creating power that intervenes in oppressive situations to restore freedom and shalom. Israel was summoned to emulate God's justice in the way she lived in the world. Sometimes she did so, but often she failed, experiencing a series of historical catastrophes in consequence.

And so the hope grew up that, one day in the future, God's liberating justice would manifest itself on earth in a new way, restoring Israel's fortunes and renewing all creation.

God's justice, incarnated in Jesus, is a liberating, community-creating power.

In the New Testament, Jesus represents the fulfillment of this biblical hope. Jesus incarnates the justice of God. In him, justice moves from heaven to earth in a new and dramatic way. For the New Testament authors, Jesus is "the just one" whose life, death, and resurrection constitute the definitive revelation of God's justice on earth (Luke 23:47; Matthew 27:19; 1 Peter 3:18; James 5:6; 1 John 2:29; Revelation 15:3; compare with Romans 1:16-17, 3:21-26). Christians, therefore, can learn most about justice from examining the life, teaching, and activity of Jesus.

49

A Mission of Justice

Jesus would have been well aware of the longstanding biblical expectation that one day God would "raise up for David a righteous Branch [to] execute justice and righteousness in the land" (Jeremiah 23:5; Isaiah 9:2-7, 11:1-5, 61:1-9). At the outset of his ministry, Jesus deliberately evoked this messianic expectation by defining his own mission in terms of bringing justice to the oppressed.

> He stood up to read, and the scroll of the prophet Isaiah was given to him. He unrolled the scroll and found the place where it was written: "The Spirit of the Lord is upon me, because he has anointed me to bring good news to the poor. He has sent me to proclaim release to the captives and recovery of sight to the blind, to let the oppressed go free, to proclaim the year of the Lord's favor." And he rolled up the scroll, gave it back to the attendant, and sat down. The eyes of all in the synagogue were fixed on him.

In his ensuing ministry, Jesus enacted this mission statement. He went about proclaiming that "the kingdom of God"—the long-awaited reign of divine justice on earth—was now getting underway (Mark 1:14-15; Matthew 4:17). He summoned his hearers to put the claims of God's royal justice ahead of all lesser concerns (Matthew 6:33). He healed the sick, fed the hungry, delivered the demonized, and challenged dominant systems of exclusion and oppression. His campaign of nonviolent justice was, for Matthew, precisely what Isaiah 42 had anticipated.

> Many crowds followed him, and he cured all of them, and he ordered them not to make him known. This was to fulfill what had been spoken through the prophet Isa-

iah: "Here is my servant, whom I have chosen, my beloved, with whom my soul is well pleased. I will put my Spirit upon him, and *he will proclaim justice to the Gentiles*. He will not wrangle or cry aloud, nor will anyone hear his voice in the streets. He will not break a bruised reed or quench a smoldering wick *until he brings justice to victory*. And in his name the Gentiles will hope" (Matthew 12:14-21; compare with Isaiah 42:1-4).

These texts contradict the prevalent image of Jesus as a spiritual teacher with little interest in politics or social change. A nonpolitical Jesus has been a basic tenet of both popular piety and much Christian scholarship for a long time. In this understanding, Jesus came as a savior, not a political activist. He proclaimed a spiritual kingdom, not an earthly kingdom. He was concerned with the salvation of souls, not the transformation of society. He called for personal holiness, not political change. Scholars and preachers alike have almost totally divorced Jesus from the concrete justice issues of his day (and therefore of our day, too).

But it is not really possible to isolate Jesus completely from the social and political issues of his time. If God's kingdom has nothing to do with the kingdoms of this world, why did the political rulers of this world destroy Jesus? (John 18:36-37) How could Jesus evoke Jewish messianic expectation without coming to terms with the political and military implications of his role? Is a nonpolitical Jesus historically credible? The answer is plainly, no.

A Kingdom Not of this World?

One of the reasons why we often miss the political character of much of Jesus' ministry is that we work with a very narrow, and a very modern, conception of what constitutes "political" activity. We come to the gospels with the modern dichotomy between church and state in our minds and think of politics in terms of Western participatory democracy. Because Jesus did not form a political party or run for office in the Sanhedrin, because he did not teach about the nature of social institutions, we conclude that he was an apolitical religious teacher who kept himself aloof from the sordid realities of political life.

But our modern distinction between religious and political life is alien to ancient Jewish society. The religious leaders of Jesus' day also exercised political power. The law of Moses was the law of the land. The Temple was the center of spiritual and civil authority, as well as the powerhouse of the Jerusalem economy. The Sanhedrin was the major arm of domestic government, and the Jerusalem authorities were finally responsible to the Roman governor. Religion and politics formed a unity in Jewish Palestine, and indeed in antiquity in general. Consequently, Jesus' conflict with the religious authorities, which looms large in the gospel accounts, was simultaneously a conflict with the centers of political power in the nation. And the issues at stake were much more to do with justice than theology.

> Jesus' mission was political as well as spiritual.

The political ramifications of Jesus' ministry did not escape his opponents. Jesus' message and lifestyle, his disregard for certain traditions and customs, his reinterpretation of the law, and especially his high-handed action in the Temple precincts, were perceived by his opponents as a challenge to the very cornerstones of Jewish society and ultimately to the Roman provincial peace (compare Luke 19:39; John 11:50). It is not surprising, then, that those most antagonistic to Jesus were those in positions of religious, political, and military power in the ruling establishment, both Jewish and Gentile. They had a vested interest in the way things were and had the most to lose from Jesus' demand for the reordering of personal and social relationships in accordance with the justice of God's coming kingdom.

A Twofold Strategy

The political stance of Jesus was characterized by a prophetic denunciation of the injustices and social evils of the surrounding society on the one hand, and by a calling together of an alternative society to live out the reality of God's kingdom on the other. This twofold strategy is evident in at least four major areas of social life addressed by Jesus.

1. A Rejection of Social Discrimination

Supremely characteristic of Jesus was his orientation to the social margins—the destitute, the weak, social outcasts, women, children, the physically deformed, the sick, and the demon-possessed. The dawning of the kingdom of God, insisted Jesus, was good news for the socially disadvantaged (Luke 4:18-22; Matthew 11:2-6; Luke 7:18-35). It brought to them both the comfort of God's acceptance despite their social exclusion, and the reassurance that God was now at work, in Jesus and his ministry, to end their suffering and restore them to community.

Jesus combated social discrimination at two levels. He openly criticized the self-righteous arrogance of the religious experts, and knowingly antagonized them by enjoying intimate fellowship with sinners and outcasts (for example, Matthew 9:13, 21:31; Luke 6:24-25, 16:15; Mark 2:15-17; Matthew 9:10-13; Luke 5:27-32; Matthew 11:19; Luke 15:1-2; Luke 19:1-10). At the same time, he assembled a new inclusive community in which the poor were to be given preference (for example, Luke 14:12-24), the sick and the imprisoned cared for (Matthew 25:31-46), women accorded dignity and equality (for example, Luke 8:1-3, 10:38-42; Mark 14:3-9, 15:40-41; John 3:7-8), children esteemed as models to be emulated (Mark 9:36,42; Matthew 18:1-5; Luke 9:46-48; Mark 10:13-16; Matthew 19:13-15; Luke 18:15-17), and Gentiles and Samaritans embraced as equal recipients of God's favor (for example, Mark 7:24-30; Matthew 15:21-28; Mark 11:17, 13:10; Matthew 8:5-13; Luke 7:1-10; Matthew 12:18, 21:43; Luke 20:16; Matthew 28:19-20; Luke 9:51-55; John 4:7-42).

2. A Critique of Economic Injustice

It is impossible to read Luke's gospel without sensing Jesus' profound hostility to materialism. As an alternative source of security, surplus wealth creates a barrier to radical trust in God (Mark 4:19; Matthew 13:22; Luke 8:14; Mark 10:17-31; Matthew 19:16-30; Luke 18:18-30; Matthew 6:21; Luke 12:16-21, 14:1-14, 16:13). Moreover, the concentration of massive riches in the hands of a few was evidence of structural injustice in society. The rich prospered at the expense of the poor. Jesus' words, "For you always have the poor with you" (Mark 14:7; Matthew 26:11; John 12:8), should not be taken as a sign of his passive acquiescence to poverty in society. His words are, in fact, an implied rebuke, for according to Deuteronomy 15:11, enduring poverty was evidence of a failure to keep the laws of the covenant.

Jesus' use of the intriguing term "dishonest wealth"—literally "mammon of injustice"—may even imply that he saw in the pursuit of wealth an inherent tendency towards injustice (Luke 16:9). This is confirmed in his overt attack on the greedy rich of his day.

Woe to you who are rich now,
for you have received your consolation.

Woe to you who are full now,
for you shall hunger (Luke 6:24-25).

Jesus criticized the wealthy elite for three related evils:
for accumulating unneeded surplus (Luke 12:15-21, 16:19,
21:1-4; Matthew 11:8), for ignoring the needs of the poor
(Luke 10:25-37, 16:19-27), and for corrupting and exploit-
ing the weak (Mark 11:15-19, 12:40; Luke 20:47; Matthew
23:23ff; Luke 11:42f). By contrast, Jesus pronounced beat-
itude upon the poor.

Blessed are you poor,
for yours is the kingdom of God.
Blessed are you who hunger,
for you shall be full.
Blessed are you who weep,
for you shall laugh (Luke 6:20-21; Matthew 5:3-12).

Jesus is *not* here turning poverty, hunger, and tears into
"spiritual values" in themselves. The poor, the starving,
and the sorrowful are not blessed because of their condition, but because God intends to *reverse* their situation.
When God's kingdom comes in its fullness, poverty and
pain will be no more. In the meantime, God's power is at
work in Jesus to bring healing and liberation and to create
a new community to work against poverty, hunger, and
misery. In this new community, a whole new attitude toward material possessions is to prevail. A lifestyle of sharing (for example, Mark 10:17-30; Matthew 6:2-4, 7:7-11;
Luke 6:35, 38, 8:1-3, 12:32-34, 19:1-10, 14:25-35; John 12:6,
13:29), simplicity (Matthew 6:19-34; Luke 12:22-31), material dependence (Mark 6:7-13; compare with Luke 9:3,
10:4), and constant vigilance against the "deceitfulness of
riches" (Mark 4:19) are to be the hallmarks of the new
community.

3. A Mistrust of Institutional Power

The ministry of Jesus was conducted in the context of an occupied country. Ultimate power resided in Rome, but indigenous rulers were allowed to exercise jurisdiction over their own territories, as long as they did so in the interests of the empire. In Jesus' day, Galilee was controlled by Herod Antipas, while Judea was controlled by a Roman governor, Pontius Pilate, although internal affairs were administered by the Jewish Sanhedrin.

As a result, Jesus was confronted by three main forms of institutional or state power: the spiritual and domestic authority of the Jewish religious leaders, the civil authority of Herod and the Herodians, and the imperial and military authority of Rome. And he was critical of all three. The basic presupposition of his political critique was that ultimate sovereignty belongs to God alone, and God's justice must be the measuring rod against which the exercise of human power is to be evaluated.

- Throughout his ministry Jesus was frequently opposed by *Jewish religious leaders.* Jesus responded to their opposition with blistering denunciations of their conduct and role in society (for example, Mark 7:6-23, 12:1-12, 41-44, 13:9-10; Luke 11:42-44, 16:14-31, 18:9-14). The most extensive example of this is found in Matthew 23. A careful reading of this chapter shows that it was not their theological views Jesus objected to; it was their misuse of religious power to entrench injustice. They used God's law to "lock people out of the kingdom of heaven" and to overburden the weak without lifting a finger to help (verses 1-4,13-16). They abused their sacred trust to accrue personal prestige and kudos (verses 5-7). They presented themselves as paragons of virtue, but were full of extortion and greed within (verse 25).

They condemned the violence of the past, but were more than ready to shed innocent blood themselves (verses 23-39). Most tellingly, they majored in legal minutiae at the expense of what matters most to God: justice, mercy, and faithfulness.

> Woe to you, scribes and Pharisees, hypocrites! For you tithe mint, dill, and cumin, and have neglected the weightier matters of the law: justice and mercy and faith. It is these you ought to have practiced without neglecting the others. You blind guides! You strain out a gnat but swallow a camel! (Matthew 23:23-24)

- The *Herodians* were also threatened by Jesus and sought to destroy him (Mark 3:6, 12:13). When some sympathetic Pharisees warn Jesus that Herod Antipas is out to kill him, Jesus sends a message of defiance back to "that fox" (Luke 13:31-33). Later when tried by Herod, he refuses to cooperate with his interrogation (Luke 23:6-12).

- Jesus was also critical of *Roman power.* It is true that Jesus never voiced direct opposition to Roman rule. He never called for the violent expulsion of the Romans from the holy land. But this does not mean that he was indifferent to Roman control or approved of it. Several considerations show he was not detached from this issue:

  1. To begin with, Jesus' proclamation of God's kingdom *presupposed* a repudiation of the Roman boast that they had already introduced the Golden Age of "peace and stability." Rome had pacified the world by force. Jesus did not regard this situation as the peace that God wanted. The Roman *Pax* was a pseudo-peace and Jesus refused to give his blessing to it (com-

pare with John 14:27, 18:36). Indeed he recognized that his mission would destabilize the present "peaceful" order because it challenged the oppression and injustice on which it was built (compare with Matthew 10:34-35; Luke 23:1-2).

2. Jesus' ethical teaching and whole manner of life also constituted an *implicit* criticism of Roman values and priorities. Jesus opts for the sick and the poor; the Romans rewarded the strong. Jesus stresses humility and service; the Romans took pride in their own superiority. Jesus stresses the sharing of surplus possessions; the Romans enacted oppressive taxes. Jesus rejects the use of the sword; the Romans specialized in violence.

3. There are also several places where Jesus *explicitly* criticizes the Roman authorities. In one saying, Jesus underlines the coercive and self-serving nature of Roman rule (Luke 22:25; compare with Mark 10:42; Matthew 20:25). In another he speaks disparagingly of the material trappings of Gentile rule and says that more respect is owed to the least in the kingdom of God than to kings and rulers (Matthew 11:8; Luke 7:25). In yet another he anticipates violence and murderous opposition to the gospel from Gentile governors and kings (Mark 13:9f; Luke 21:12f; compare with Matthew 24:9). Jesus' most important statement on Roman authority occurs in the so-called Tribute Question.

Then they sent to him some Pharisees and some Herodians to trap him in what he said. And they came and said to him, "Teacher, we know that you are sincere, and show deference to no one; for you do not regard people with partiality, but teach the way of God in accordance with truth. Is it lawful to pay taxes to the emperor, or not? Should we pay them, or should we not?" But knowing their hypocrisy, he said to them, "Why are you putting me to the test? Bring me a denarius and let me see it." And they brought one. Then he said to them, "Whose head is this, and whose title?" They answered, "The emperor's." Jesus said to them, "Give to the emperor the things that are the emperor's, and to God the things that are God's." And they were utterly amazed at him (Mark 12:13-17; Matthew 22:15-22; Luke 20:20-26).

In saying, "Give to the emperor the things that are the emperor's, and to God the things that are God's," Jesus was not seeking to distinguish between our spiritual and political responsibilities, and prioritizing the former. Nor was he condoning imperial taxation in principle. (If his words were intended as an unambiguous affirmation of Rome's right to levy taxes, it is hard to see how his enemies could construe them as sedition [Luke 23:2].) Instead, sidestepping the specific issue of taxation, Jesus pointed his questioners to a deeper underlying principle—namely that the demands of the Roman emperor must be critically evaluated in light of the demands of God. All things belong to God, and only insofar as the demands of Caesar are consistent with the justice of God, may they be regarded as legitimate.

As well as speaking critically of the abusive use of power in surrounding society, Jesus taught his discipleship community to turn prevailing patterns of power and greatness upside down. In their community, there is to be no hierarchy of status, as prevailed in the contemporary religious community (Matthew 23:8-12). There is to be no domination of the weak by the powerful, no lording it over one another in the manner of Gentile rulers (Mark 10:42-43). True greatness is shown by striving to be of least account (Mark 9:33-37; Matthew 18:1-6; Luke 9:46-48; Mark 10:13-16; Matthew 19:13-15; Luke 18:15-17). Leadership is servanthood (Luke 22:26).

4. A Repudiation of War and Violence

Jesus knew that the existing "system" sanctioned violence to achieve its ends. He was well aware of the brutality of Roman rule. He spoke of Pilate's ruthlessness (Luke 13:1), and of how the Romans domineered their subjects (Luke 22:24-27). He knew he himself would eventually face torture and death at Roman hands (Mark 10:33-34; Matthew 20:17-19; Luke 18:31-34), and that his followers also faced the prospect of persecution (Mark 13:9-10; Luke 21:12-13) and crucifixion (Mark 8:34-38). He spoke gravely of the time ahead when the Romans would employ the dreadful horror of siege warfare against Jerusalem (Luke 19:41 44, 21:20 24, 23:27-31). He also knew the violence that seethed beneath the surface of Jewish society (Matthew 23:29-36; Luke 9:7-9, 19, 13:31-35; Mark 13:9-13). Jesus was no starry-eyed idealist when it came to the subject of violence.

Aware that the established order would use lethal force to oppose his work, Jesus had three existing options. He could take the *revolutionary option* of the Zealots and strive to bring in the kingdom by military force. He could take the *withdrawal option* of the Essenes and advocate a retreat into the desert, away from the corruption of surrounding society. Or he could take the *establishment option* of the

Temple rulers and seek to make the best of a poor situation by collaborating and compromising with the existing unjust order.

Jesus rejected all three. Instead, he chose the way of nonviolent, sacrificial, peacemaking love and required the same of his followers (Matthew 5:38-48). Jesus totally rejected war and violence as having any place in the pursuit of God's justice on earth.

But this did not spare Jesus from suffering a violent death himself. So threatened were those in positions of power by Jesus' message of radical love under the rule of God that they conspired to kill him.

Death and Resurrection

The New Testament depicts the death of Jesus as *both* a hideous example of human injustice *and* as a demonstration of God's saving justice. Both dimensions must be held together.

Jesus' death was both an example of injustice *and* a demonstration of God's justice. The injustice dimension is underlined in texts that attribute Jesus' arrest and execution to the powers of evil, operating through human malice in general and the self-interest of the ruling authorities in particular. Mark, for example, frequently comments on how fear, resentment, and jealousy motivated Jewish opposition (see, for example, Mark 3:6, 12:12-13, 14:1-3, 10-11, 15:10; compare with 1:22, 2:7, 6:3, 7:1-5, 8:11-21; Luke 23:48; John 19:12). Luke attributes the betrayal of Jesus to Satan entering Judas (Luke 22:3; compare with 22:31), and aligns the temple authorities who seize Jesus in Gethsemane with "the power of darkness" (Luke

22:53; compare with 23:45). John also ascribes Jesus' betrayal to Satan entering the heart of Judas (John 13:2, 27). Under the influence of its evil "ruler" (John 14:30), the world in general hated Jesus without cause (John 15:18, 25), for people "loved darkness" and "their deeds were evil" (John 3:19; compare with 1:9-11).

The speeches in Acts frequently accuse the Jewish leaders of having "betrayed," "rejected," "murdered," "condemned," and "crucified" Jesus despite his complete innocence (Acts 2:23, 36, 3:13-15, 4:10, 26-28, 7:51-52, 13:27-29; compare with Luke 23:14, 20, 22; 23:47). Paul also notes the involvement of the Jews (1 Thessalonians 2:14-15) and "the rulers of this age" (1 Corinthians 2:8; compare with Colossians 2:14) in the killing of Jesus. The writer to the Hebrews speaks more generally of Jesus enduring "hostility from sinners" (Hebrew 12:2,3), and 1 Peter speaks of him being "rejected by human beings" (1 Peter 2:4-7).

Yet Jesus' death is presented as more than an act of brutal injustice. It is also portrayed as the means by which God's saving justice defeats the power of sin and death once for all (see, for example, Romans 1:16-17, 3:21-26, 5:6-11, 8:1-4; Galatians 3:13; 1 Corinthians 15:3-4; 2 Corinthians 5:19-21; Philippians 2:6-11). In the person of Jesus, God entered fully into the experience of alienated humanity in order to break the power of evil that locks the human race into the endless cycle of violence and counter-violence. On the cross, Jesus absorbed in his own bodily experience the full impact of human sinfulness. "He himself bore our sins in his body on the cross, so that, free from sins, we might live for righteousness" (1 Peter 2:24). Jesus became the supreme victim of the violence of evil. Yet in his victimized state, Jesus did *not* perpetuate the reign of sin by retaliating against his abusers. He did not respond to violence with violence; he refused Peter's offer of a sword to defend him (Matthew 26:52). He did not respond to hatred with counter-hatred. "When he was abused, he did not return abuse; when he suffered, he did not threaten; but he entrusted himself to the one who judges justly" (1 Peter 2:23; see also Hebrews 12:2). He did not respond to victimization with vengeance. Instead he prayed for his killers: "Father, forgive them for they do not know what they are doing" (Luke 23:34).

In responding this way, Jesus reversed the logic of evil, thus crippling its power. He died a violent death. But God raised him from the dead, demonstrating that God's power is greater even than the annihilation of death that comes from the exercise of violence. Jesus' resurrection serves as objective evidence that evil has been defeated, and a new form of human existence has been initiated.

Summary

Jesus' proclamation of the kingdom of God impinged directly on the major dimensions of social and political life: the use of wealth and power, the exclusion of the weak and disadvantaged from full participation in community, and the use of lethal violence to protect the unjust status quo. Jesus was critical of the injustices of the prevailing social order and called for communal repentance.

He also laid down a new ethic for his followers. In his community, the weak are to be honored, wealth is to be justly distributed, leadership is to take the form of servanthood, and the way of nonviolent peacemaking is to prevail. Seeking to live in accordance with the vision of the coming reign of God's justice is to be the supreme concern of its existence (Matthew 6:33).

Through his death and resurrection, Jesus finally brought "justice to victory" (Matthew 12:20). The power of sin, which generates injustice in the world, was broken, enabling former "slaves of sin" now to become "slaves of righteousness"; that is, instruments of God's saving, restoring, peacemaking justice in the world (Romans 6:15-20).

> For the kingdom of God is not food and drink but righteousness and peace and joy in the Holy Spirit. The one who thus serves Christ is acceptable to God and has human approval. Let us then pursue what makes for peace and for mutual upbuilding (Romans 14:17-19).

This verse captures well what we have discovered about biblical justice and righteousness throughout this *Little Book*. Justice is the heart of God's kingdom, the way in which God exercises loving rule in the world. It is the primary obligation placed on God's people, who are called to be living witnesses to the transforming character of God's justice. It is the way we serve Christ in the world, who interprets for us most powerfully what justice means in practice. And it is in thus serving Christ that we find acceptance with God.

To strive for the justice of God's kingdom is to pursue "what makes for peace." The pursuit of justice is also what builds up the mutual bonds of community and brings joy in the Holy Spirit. For biblical justice is, finally, a joyful justice, not a grim justice. It is joyful because it restores, heals, and makes things right.

Appendix:
Summary of Key Points

- Justice is a difficult concept to define adequately, and disagreements are common about how the principle of justice translates into practice.

- Attaining justice involves the exercise of legitimate power to ensure that benefits and penalties are distributed fairly in society, and to uphold the rights and obligations of all parties.

- The biblical narrative of God's creative, sustaining, and redemptive activity is the primary place Christians can learn about the meaning of justice. Justice is a central theme in the Bible.

- Biblical teaching on justice must be understood within the religious and cultural worldview of the biblical authors. Covenant, law, and justice are overlapping and interdependent concepts in the Bible.

- God is the objective source of justice. Justice originates in God's own being and determines all of God's interactions with the world. God holds all peoples responsible for doing what justice requires.

- True knowledge of God entails understanding God's own devotion to justice and striving to emulate God's justice in one's own manner of living in the world.

- God's promise to move history in the direction of final deliverance from the blight of evil is the ground of biblical hope. Believers are called to join with God in this work of redemption and renewal.

- When measured against the perfect justice of God's coming rule, every human attempt to create justice must be seen as partial and flawed. No existing political or economic system is above critique or improvement.

- Justice doesn't happen by accident. It always requires struggle, commitment, and dedication. Because of God's commitment to justice, there is always hope for change.

- Without the commitment to seek justice, all other means of worshipping God are bankrupt. A lifestyle of justice is the essential mark of holiness.

- The accent of biblical justice falls on positive action in order to resist the oppressor and set the oppressed free.

- Those in positions of authority in society are most responsible for the pursuit of justice, although all members of the community are also subject to this demand.

- Biblical justice is all about creating and sustaining healthy, constant, and life-giving relationships between parties. Kindness and mercy are therefore essential to achieving justice.

- Biblical justice involves showing a definite partiality for the welfare of those groups in society who are most vulnerable to exploitation. God sides with the poor and weak in order to secure greater equity in society.

- When wrongdoing occurs, the fundamental concern of biblical justice is restitution and restoration of what has been damaged. Punishment often serves as a mechanism for protecting and restoring shalom.

- Jesus defined his own historical mission in terms of bringing justice to the poor and oppressed. His message represented a threat to the existing powers, which is why they opposed him.

- Jesus was fiercely critical of the abuse of political and religious power, the marginalizing of the poor and weak, and reliance on lethal violence.

- Jesus' death is a hideous example of human injustice. But it is also the definitive demonstration of God's saving and forgiving justice. Jesus' resurrection demonstrates the victory of God's justice over the powers of evil.

- The vision of God's coming kingdom is to be the supreme concern of the new messianic community. The church must embody in its own life the characteristics of justice made known in the life and activity of Jesus.

Scripture Index

Scripture Index

Scripture Index

Selected Readings

Some Relevant Books

Carter, Warren. *Matthew and the Margins: A Sociopolitical and Religious Reading* (Maryknoll, NY: Orbis, 2000).

Epzstein, Léon. *Social Justice in the Ancient Near East and the People of the Bible* (London: SCM, 1986).

Haugen, Gary A. *Good News About Injustice: A Witness of Courage in a Hurting World* (Downers Grove, IL: InterVarsity Press, 1999).

Herzog II, William R. *Jesus, Justice and the Reign of God: A Ministry of Liberation* (Louisville, KY: Westminster John Knox, 1999).

Kaylor, R. David. *Jesus the Prophet: His Vision of the Kingdom on Earth* (Louisville, KY: Westminster John Knox, 1995).

Leech, Kenneth. *True God: An Exploration in Spiritual Theology* (London: Sheldon Press, 1985).

Malchow, Bruce V. *Social Justice in the Hebrew Bible: What Is New and What Is Old* (Collegeville: Michael Glazier, 1996).

Weinfeld, Moshe. *Social Justice in Ancient Israel and in the Ancient Near East* (Minneapolis: Augsburg Fortress Press, 1995).

Wright, Christopher J.H. *An Eye for an Eye: The Place of Old Testament Ethics Today* (Downers Grove, IL: InterVarsity Press, 1983).

———. *Walking in the Ways of the Lord: The Ethical Authority of the Old Testament* (Downers Grove, IL: InterVarsity Press, 1996).

Yoder, Perry B. *Shalom: The Bible's Word for Salvation, Justice and Peace* (Newton, KS: Faith and Life Press, 1987).

Selected Readings

Related Books by Chris Marshall

Kingdom Come: the Kingdom of God in the Teaching of Jesus (Auckland: Impetus Publications, 1993).

Beyond Retribution: A New Testament Vision for Justice, Crime and Punishment (Grand Rapids, MI: Wm B. Eerdmans, 2001).

Crowned with Glory and Honor: Human Rights in the Biblical Tradition (Telford, PA: Cascadia Publishing House, 2002).

About the Author

Chris Marshall is a theological educator in New Zealand, with a special interest in community-based justice alternatives. His focus has been on the integration of theological insights and criminal justice theory in his published work, for which he has received international recognition. He has also been highly involved in a voluntary capacity in the development of restorative justice practice in New Zealand. In 2004 he received an International Community Justice Award for his work in this area.

Dr. Marshall holds the St. John's Senior Lectureship in Christian Theology at Victoria University in Wellington, New Zealand. His Ph.D. in New Testament is from the University of London. He also holds an M.A. in Peace Studies from the Associated Mennonite Biblical Seminary in Elkhart, Indiana. In addition to many articles on biblical and ethical themes, he is author of *Faith as a Theme in Mark's Narrative; Kingdom Come: The Kingdom of God in the Teaching of Jesus; Crowned with Glory and Honor: Human Rights in the Biblical Tradition;* and *Beyond Retribution: A New Testament Vision for Justice, Crime and Punishment.*

METHOD OF PAYMENT

❒ Check or Money Order
   *(payable to **Good Books** in U.S. funds)*

❒ Please charge my:
   ❒ MasterCard   ❒ Visa
   ❒ Discover   ❒ American Express

\# _____

exp. date _____

Signature _____

Name _____

Address _____

City _____

State _____

Zip _____

Phone _____

Email _____

SHIP TO: (if different)

Name _____

Address _____

City _____

State _____

Zip _____

Mail order to: **Good Books**
P.O. Box 419 • Intercourse, PA 17534-0419
Call toll-free: 800/762-7171
Fax toll-free: 888/768-3433
Prices subject to change.

Group Discounts for

The Little Book of Biblical Justice
ORDER FORM

If you would like to order multiple copies of *The Little Book of Biblical Justice* by Chris Marshall for groups you know or are a part of, use this form. (Discounts apply only for more than one copy.)
Photocopy this page as often as you like.

The following discounts apply:

1 copy	$4.95
2-5 copies	$4.45 each (a 10% discount)
6-10 copies	$4.20 each (a 15% discount)
11-20 copies	$3.96 each (a 20% discount)
21-99 copies	$3.45 each (a 30% discount)
100 or more	$2.97 each (a 40% discount)

Free shipping for U.S. orders of 100 or more!
Prices subject to change.

Quantity   *Price*   *Total*

_____ copies of *Biblical Justice*   @ _____ _____

Shipping & Handling
(U.S. orders only: add 10%; $3.95 minimum) _____
For international orders, please call 800/762-7171, ext. 221

PA residents add 6% sales tax _____

TOTAL _____
